<u>Dedication</u>

I want to thank my mom for always supporting and believing in me. I want her to know all of her prayers over my life have never been taken for granted.

I want to thank my dad for his tough love while growing up as a child. I know without a doubt I would not be the man I am today without him in my life.

I witnessed my mom create her own wedding business. She was so happy working for herself and doing what she loved.

I witnessed my father create his own mortgage and commercial cleaning business. It gave him the freedom to do what he loved to do, which was coach.

Both of my parents inspired me to find a way to make money by doing something I love to do.

Last but not least, this book is dedicated to anyone who has faced adversity in life and never gave up. I salute you all. Keep going and never stop. I'm proud of you!

Contents

Foreword – Dr. Randy Bell

Chapter 1 - What is wholesale real estate?

- Definition
- Cold Calling
- Common Questions & Responses
- Potential Motivated Seller

Chapter 2 – Verify The Deal

- Serious Motivated Seller
- Determining ARV
- 1% Rule
- Five Big Ticket Items
- Determining The Seller Offer

Chapter 3 - Four Reasons For Selling

- Debt
- Divorce
- Death
- Disaster

Chapter 4 - How To Find A Deal?

- Purchase Leads
- Skip Trace
- Call Leads
- Identify Motivated Seller
- Put Under Contract
- Clear Title
- Find Buyer
- Close The Deal

Chapter 5 - Contract Agreements

- Purchase and Sale Agreement With Seller
- Assignment of Contract
- Purchase and Sale Agreement With Buyer
- Joint Venture Agreement
- Marketing Agreement

FOREWORD

If you are thinking about pursuing a career in Real Estate, then you are thinking correct. Picture a choose-your-adventure novel in which the sky is the limit. I know it sounds cliché, but hard work and dedication still go a long way. You have to start somewhere but only you can choose how you keep going. Everyone needs somewhere to live and by working in this powerful industry, you have the ability to arm yourself with direct methods to help find the perfect roof to put over your clients head. Or in some cases help them get into a better situation with the sale of their property. The most important thing to understand about business is that business is simply a matter of your systems and processes (how you create more business and how you handle the business once it comes in). The more automated you can become, the quicker you can scale. Go hard or go home and lock yourself inside because if you are outside, you better be working smart! Study Long, Study Wrong...

Dr. Randy Bell
Licensed Texas Realtor

Chapter 1.

What is Wholesale Real Estate?

"Wholesale Real Estate Is The Old Rich White Man Hustle"

What is Wholesale Real Estate? "A real estate wholesaler executes a contract with a home seller, markets the contract to the property to potential end buyers, and assigns the contract to the buyer. The wholesaler makes a profit – called the "assignment fee," which is the difference between the contracted price with the seller and the amount paid by the end buyer." - *Reference 1.*

We have been programmed to believe the only way you can buy or sell a home is the traditional route by using a realtor or broker. For a real estate novice who wants to sell or buy a home, using a Realtor or Broker is the best route to use. They are licensed professionals who will walk their clients through the entire transaction. However, most people are not aware that they can buy or sell their home without using the traditional route. Everyone knows that Real Estate is a great business to be in. I want to introduce you another side of the Real Estate business called Wholesale Real Estate. Wholesale Real Estate is the old rich white man hustle that they do not teach you. WHOLESALE REAL ESTATE IS COMPLETELY LEGAL! The best thing about Wholesale is that any person who is of legal age (18 years old) to sign a legally binding contract can wholesale Real Estate. Wholesale does not require a license or special certification. However, it does require you to study your local state laws that govern all real estate transactions. It is wise to gain thorough knowledge of how real estate contracts are written. Wholesale real estate thrives on one of America's most essential values, which is freedom of choice. A homeowner has the legal right to sell his or her home to anyone who has the money to buy it. All that is needed are the four simple steps below.

(1.) Purchase and sale agreement (PSA) between two parties

(2.) Submit the PSA to a title attorney office to ensure clear title records

(3.) Transfer funds into title escrow account,

(4.) Sign closing documents and the deal is done

Savvy Real Estate investors take advantage of this knowledge by not depending on listing platforms such as MLS, Zillow, and Redfin, Realtor.com etc to find deals. Savvy Real Estate investors love exclusive deals, which are usually, considered "Off Market" listings. Typically they find these deals from family or friends who may know someone who wants to sell a home in the future. Most times investors depend on getting properties from a wholesaler. Many people are unfamiliar with the term "Wholesale Real Estate". However, people are marketing wholesale real estate everyday and you didn't even notice. For example, everyone has seen those signs that say "We Buy Houses" with a telephone number underneath. Not to mention those annoying video ads that interrupts your favorite pod-cast or music video saying " Want to learn how to buy real estate with no money down? Click the link below and get started today." All of that is wholesale real estate and you didn't even know. Before we go any further, if you think I'm about to say you can become a millionaire in six months doing wholesale real estate. Stop reading. I am definitely not going to feed you a false dream. Nor will I say you have to quit your job that supports your family to make this work. Nope, you won't hear that from me. However, I will say, the more time you dedicate to anything, the more you learn and more success you will have. Now that we have got that out of the way, lets talk about the fun stuff, cold calling.

Cold Calling

Depending on your personality this may not be so fun. But let me state that cold calling is BY FAR the most effective way to get the BEST deals & make the most money. No one really does door knocking for Real Estate deals anymore. Some may say "Driving for dollars" is very lucrative too. For those who may not know what driving for dollars is, here is a quick definition. Driving for dollars means driving in a neighborhood looking for abandoned or vacant homes, writing down the addresses then looking up the owner's information to contact them to inquire if they would be interested in selling. Now lets get back to cold calling. Cold Calling is sales at its finest and is the best way to sharpen your negotiation skills in real time. If you don't mind having people hang up, scream, curse or tell you to get a real job, you will do fine cold calling. A director of mine once told me that sales is nothing more than getting through all the "No's" just to get to the one "Yes". That is the mindset I suggest anyone to have. One yes could turn into $500 or $44k. I used the amounts $500 or $44k because my first payment in Real Estate was $500 and my biggest payment was $44k. I split this $44k payment with my good friend and business partner Charles Drinkard III (now Licensed Texas Realtor). We made $22k each and got the deal from making cold calls. Another attractive thing about doing your own cold calls is that other people hate to do it, and most people aren't good at it. So it's a great market to be in if you're a shark like myself. Here are some of the most common questions and responses you will run into from potential motivated sellers (PMS), when you ask if they are interested in selling a property.

1.) How much will you give me?

2.) How did you get my number?

3.) Who do you work for?

4.) Maybe in the future

5.) No

6.) Yes

How much will you give me?

This question could mean a couple things from the PMS standpoint. It could mean they have been receiving calls about the property and want to know how your offer compares to their other offers. They could be fishing to see if you have a serious offer and not just someone looking to low ball them. It could also mean they have no clue what their property is worth and want to know how much you're willing to offer them. Here is free game. During the initial conversation do not make a solid offer on any property you have not seen both inside and outside of the property. Instead say something along the lines of "I would like to give you a solid offer once I have had the chance to run comps and take a look inside of the property". This will usually lead to either them to giving you a date you can visit the property or lead to them giving you an estimate how much they are willing to take.

How did you get my number?

This is the easiest question to respond too and so many new beginners in cold calling get caught up on this one. Simply, tell the truth by saying, "your number is in public records in the city and county you own properties in". This is a true statement. There are multiple personal data websites that you can pay a monthly subscription for to get homeowners contact numbers and email address. The best companies to use are Transunion TLOxp & LexisNexis. They have the most accurate data and are the hardest to get approved for due to the accuracy of their data. Accurate numbers for a PMS is a very essential part of your success. Without accurate numbers, you will be wasting your time cold calling wrong numbers and will never see the results needed to be successful in wholesale real estate.

Who do you work for?

You're probably asking yourself, why would someone want to know who do you work for? Please understand the people you call may also be investors and most get tons a call a day from other wholesalers. These investors are typically looking to see if you're an independent investor, wholesaler or employed by an acquisitions company. Here is a good answer for you to use "I work for (Name of your company) & we have investors in our network who are specifically looking for homes to purchase in (City Name) Metro Area. Remember less is more. You want them to do more talking than you & the goal is to find out if they are looking to sell. Then most importantly finding out why they do or do not want to sell.

Maybe In The Future

This is a person you immediately add to your follow up lead sheet as a warm lead. Remember that $44k deal I mentioned earlier? It started off with a "maybe in the future" response too. For 9 months straight, I called that warm lead once a month. Then one day their response changed from maybe to yes we are ready to sell. "The Fortune Is In The Follow Up" is a phrase Randy Bell (now Licensed Realtor in Texas) would often say when he first introduced me to Wholesale Real Estate in 2017. Trust me do your follow ups because regretting you didn't follow up and missing out on a great deal does not feel so good. The fortune as you know is the $44k deal. The regret is forgetting to call every month and finding out later they sold the property a month before you decided to call them back. This happened to me a couple of times when I first started. I vowed to NEVER let a warm lead get away again.

NO.

No is never the answer we are looking for and some people will say no then hang up or not say anything then hang up. Do not call them back. Move on to the next lead. On the other hand some people may respond saying no but you can hear they don't know why they are saying no. It is important for you to understand that you are offering a service to put money in a homeowner pocket if they agree to sell. That must be leveraged in your conversations with each seller. Find out what is going on in their life and why it would benefit them to sell. We will go into details about the Four D's in a later chapter, but you must find out what is going on personally with the seller and empathize with them while pitching why selling their home is a great idea for their current situation.

It is important to have a shark mentality when doing business. For an example, if I know the condition of their home is abandoned. No, is an unacceptable answer. I will market myself as someone who cares about the community who doesn't want to see abandoned homes bringing down the value of my beloved community. People tend to want to sell their property to someone who cares. It is important to realize the seller is not only selling the home for money but they are also selling to the person they think you are. People do business with people they like. You must have personality on every call.

In addition, if they have outstanding tax debt owed to the city (yes, you can look that up free of charge). That is another incentive to encourage them to sell.

Remember in wholesale real estate you make the most money on the worst home in the neighborhood. Usually this house has a financial issue attached.

YES.

This is the entire reason we make these calls and it is very important that you know what next steps you need to do when you get a PMS willing to sell. This takes us to the next chapter "Verify The Deal".

Chapter 2.

Verify The Deal

"Always Run Your Numbers First"

Identifying a potential motivated seller (PMS) is just the beginning. Now you must determine if they are a serious motivated seller (SMS). First you must verify a list of things before putting the property under contract and marketing to your buyers. It is important to understand how to determine the current market value "as is" and the after repair value (ARV). This will help your negotiations when you began to discover the reason PMS wants to sell their home. I will discuss the main reasons most sellers want to sell their home in the next chapter. For now let's focus on determining the current market value. This can be done by looking at homes with similar square foot, lot size, year build & within 0.25 – 0.5 radius of the property your PMS is looking to sell. The easiest way to determine current market value and ARV is to look at homes sold within the last year that are comparable to your PMS home. Most end buyers want to see three solid comparable (comps) homes and low DOM (Days On Market) usually less than 30 days. This will give you a starting point on how much you can sell the property to your end buyer. Knowing how much your end buyer wants to pay and ensuring they get their return on investment is key to building a successful relationship with your end buyers.

You need to make sure you get an asking price from your PMS. Most motivated sellers will have an asking price. It is very important to get them to give you a number first. The reason for this is because you don't want to waste your time with a PMS that asking price is too high for the current "as is" condition its in. Once you get their asking price make sure you determine if it is vacant or occupied. You can ask if the home is vacant or occupied prior to getting their asking price. If the home is occupied the PMS must be renting at or close current rental market value to be attractive to your end buyers. Most end buyers don't like buying homes at current market value with a tenant in a lease paying under current market rent. I suggest you learn the 1% Rule when attempting to sell an occupied property. Below are three key points regarding the 1% Rule (Reference #2)

- The rent charged should be equal to or greater than the investor's mortgage payment to ensure that they at least break even on the property
- Multiply the purchase price of the property plus any necessary repairs by 1% to determine a base level of monthly rent
- Ideally, an investor should seek a mortgage loan with monthly payments of less than the 1% figure

If the property is occupied you must find out how much rent the tenant is paying and how long their lease is or if the tenant is month to month. Also you need to know if the tenant is on section 8 or not. This information is important to what buyer you need to market this property to. The next thing you need to do, whether its tenant occupied or vacant, is request access into the property. You must gain access to assess the condition of the property. This information will help determine your offer price. There are a few key big-ticket items you need to inspect and/or inquire about when you schedule a visit the property.

1.) Foundation

2.) Roofing

3.) Plumbing

4.) HVAC/ Central Air & Heat

5.) Electricity (If no HVAC, then Electricity updated will be required.)

All of the items above need to be inspected during your visit. Most are visible to the eyes, especially foundation issues and roofing problems. It would help to befriend a general contractor who can give you free quotes on the estimated repair cost (ERC). This will not only give you accurate ERC but also put you ahead of your peer competitors. After the inspection you should review the comps again and prepare to make an offer.

Determining the seller offer and how much a buyer will be willing to pay for the property takes some simple math. Lets say you have a SMS whose property after repair value (ARV) is $100,000. Most investors use the 70% rule when buying real estate properties to flip. The 70% rule states real estate investors shouldn't pay more than 70% of the ARV minus the repairs needed. If a house is $100,000 and needs $40,000 in repairs, the 70% rule states not more than $30,000 should be paid.

The math looks like this: (Reference #3)

- $100,000 (ARV) x .70 (ARV Percentage) = $70,000
- $70,000 – $40,000 (ERC) = $30,000 (Buying Price)

If you can successfully get your SMS to sign a purchase and sales agreement for $15k - $20k & assign your contract to your investor for $30k. Then you will net a $10k - $15k profit. This is how you profit from real estate without using any money down, or having a credit check. This is known as wholesale real estate. This is the real estate secret they don't teach you.

Chapter 3.

Four Reasons For Selling

"Find Their Pain"

When I first started Real Estate I struggled trying to figure out how to understand which sellers were truly motivated on my warm leads. So I would prioritize every lead and literally exhaust myself with negotiations daily. One day a guy who was much more experienced in real estate said to me, "Cedric there are only four reasons someone wants to sell their home. Finding out which of these four reasons should be your primary goal on every call". When I applied this method to my strategy, identifying the SMS was no longer a struggle.

Four Main Reasons a seller wants to sell (4 D's)

1.) Debt

2.) Divorce

3.) Death

4.) Disaster

All four are major triggers for most people. Using these 4 D's allows us to determine who is a SMS or who is just a PMS. A potential motivated seller usually is not looking to sell unless you make a good offer. On the other hand, a serious motivated seller is in a position that they MUST sell. Those are the sellers you want to prioritize on your warm leads sheet.

Debt

Lets discuss SMS with debt issues. There are a multitude of reasons people will have debt issues. For example, many vacant/abandoned homes are behind on city taxes. These tax bills can add up to a very high amount for a home no one lives in anymore and most of the family is out of state. Sometimes the taxes owed are more than what the property is worth. In that case, if you can't get the city to agree to reduce the taxes, it's best to move onto the next deal. The most popular reason debt affects seller to having to sell their home quickly is due to threat of foreclosure. These are the best ones because they ABSOLUTELY have to sell. Banks consider home mortgage a dead asset and would much rather work with an end buyer who can fund a large sum of the amount owed.

Something you should know as you began to wholesale properties is that you will learn how to do a Real Estate transaction from start to finish. Most end buyers do not seek FMLS listed properties (properties listed by realtors). Real Estate Investors like exclusive deals that not every other investor has viewed or has placed a bid on. However, they do use their personal realtors to list their rehabbed properties.

Quick Motivational Interlude:

"I want to stress that you must enjoy the learning process. It doesn't matter how many books you read or seminars you attend, you will only get better by actually doing the work. Do not be afraid of failure, because in this business it is inevitable to fail. Never quit until you reach your goals. I find it satisfying knowing that I can earn a living for myself without having to depend on a company. If you have a fulltime job, find YOUR balance, live your life the best you can. Ok, enough motivation for now, lets get back to the business."

Divorce

Divorce settlement can be both brutal and profitable. It is definitely profitable for any wholesaler who is aware of properties that will be sold due to a recent divorce. Knowing divorce lawyers will serve your business well if you take advantage of your resources. During most divorces we know the couples martial home will most likely be sold in "as is" condition since both parties want to eliminate their financial obligation to one another as soon as possible. Some people may say this is harsh or you should not look to profit during the time when people are having a hard moment in life. My response is, "Do the hospitals take the same consideration for their cancer patients? Do insurance companies lower their rates for people with known health issues? Do car repair shops work on vehicles free after someone has been in an accident? Are the towing companies free of charge? Are court fees and legal counsel free during a divorce?" I can go on and on, but the simple answer is that majority of America's booming businesses are built around people hardships and the unfortunate truth is that business/industries make a lot of money during crisis in people lives.

Death

We have all experienced the loss of a loved one and it's one of the most common time families seek to sell a relative home due to funeral expenses, avoiding paying yearly taxes on a home no one lives in anymore etc. While you are making your calls you will come across people who will say the person you called to speak with is no longer living. This is the time you ask the hard question, "Would you be interested in selling?" Most will say they have not thought much about it or simply no or yes. Death is hard for most people to deal with and these cases must be worked with extreme patience. Remember the $44k deal I closed with my partner Charles, well that was this exact scenario. The reason it took 9 months for them to finally agree to sell is because the seller husband committed suicide in that home and the home was where they raised their family. Understand that there is no price tag on sentimental value. Only time can change people minds in those cases.

Disaster

Hurricane, tornadoes, earthquakes, the list goes on and on. Every year there is a major disaster that strikes a city or town. Government-funded programs such as FEMA usually support these disasters. I told you earlier businesses thrive during crisis. There is no bigger disaster besides death that is more heartbreaking than losing your home during a storm. Disasters are the main reason people sell homes they would not have sold in any other circumstance.

Disasters also come in the form of sickness. Most people will put themselves in serious debt to help a love one who is very ill. Being sick is not cheap, and can get very expensive which becomes a tremendous financial disaster for most working class people. We all know the treatment facilities are not free and are very costly. A wholesaler is very beneficial to a SMS who's love one is sick and need to sell a home in "as is" condition to help cover the medical bills. Typically they need a quick closing and simple contracts. You will have the opportunity to help a family get fair market value for their property and give your investor a great property while making a profit for yourself.

Identifying the 4 D's in each call with your PMS are essential to the success of your business. Use this information as a guide as you navigate through your real estate journey. I do not recommend taking advantage by offering unreasonable low-ball offers to people during these times. Most time people will know your offer isn't good and will no longer answer your call. Always offer fair market value based on the "as is" condition of the home. Always treat people well and those same people will likely refer you to another family or friend. Treating people fair is always the right thing to do.

Chapter 4.

How To Find A Deal?

"The Right Information Is Key To Economic Success"

Everyone wants to know the answer to this one question when they began their real estate career, "Where do I find leads"? Below are the eight steps to completing a wholesale transaction.

1.) Purchase Leads

2.) Skip Trace

3.) Call Leads

4.) Identify Motivated Seller

5.) Put under contract

6.) Clear title

7.) Find buyer

8.) Close the deal

Step 1.) Purchase Leads

There are many websites you can purchase leads from but my favorite is Melissa.com. I use Melissa.com because they target the absentee homeowners.

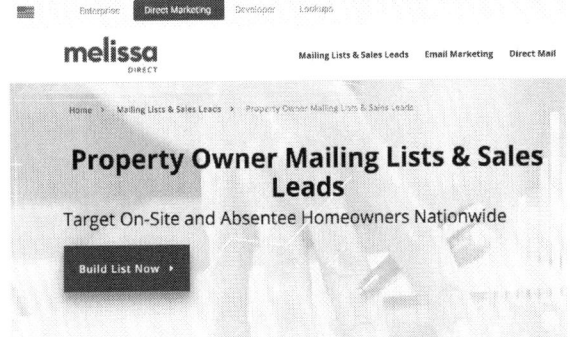

Absentee homeowners are people who have homes in their name that is not their primary residents. This is important because now you know the person you are calling is likely familiar with real estate and they usually have more than one property. I cannot express how much money I have made off a couple calls that turned out to be a real estate investor who had 30+ properties. I literally survived an entire year working one investor portfolio that I got from cold calling.

Step 2.) Skip Trace

Now this can be tricky, but for the most accurate numbers will be from Tlo & LexisNexis.

https://www.tlo.com/

Right data.
Better results.
Right now.

https://www.lexisnexis.com/

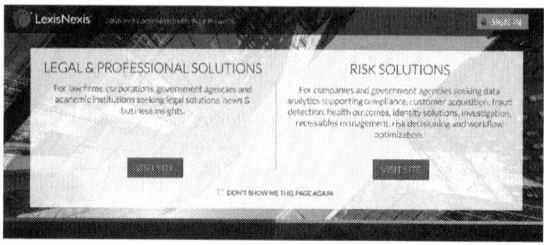

A great alternative is to hire a contractor who will skip trace the leads for you. If you have never hired a contractor I suggest using Fiverr.com. This is probably the greatest gift to any business owner who needs work done at reasonable cost.

https://www.fiverr.com/

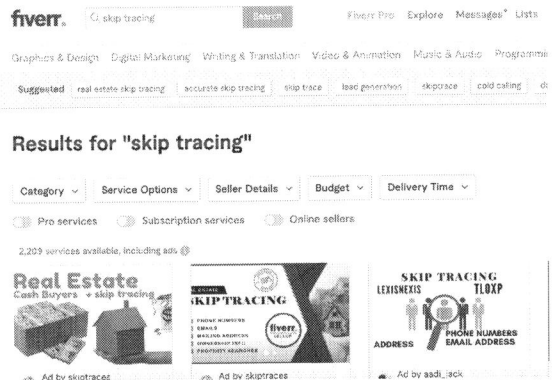

They are the number one outsource network in my opinion. Simply type in the search bar "skip trace" and dozens for people looking for work will appear. Carefully read the reviews. I usually like to start with the bad reviews first. Just so I can get some balance besides all the glorified "They are amazing to work with" 5 star comments. People with the most reviews are typically more dependable.

Step 3.) Call Leads

I highly suggest calling your leads to get a grasp of what you're doing in this business. If you plan to scale your business and have people work under you then you definitely need to be banging out minimum 200 leads a day. Notice I said leads, not calls because most time when you hire someone to skip trace your leads they will give you between 3-7 numbers for each lead.

![LA LEADS COMPLETED.xlsx spreadsheet screenshot]

So yes, you need to be calling 200 leads a day when you first start. After you have had some success on deals and want to focus more on building your end buyers list, I suggest hiring virtual assistants (VA's).

Free Game

I intentionally did not highlight the virtual assistant (VA) as a step for this chapter. This is information is for the people who actually read the book or just got lucky and landed on this page. Either way, this information will transcend your business from the daily grind into an automated business model. Lets get into the good stuff now. I personally like to use www.onlinePH.com as seen on the screenshot below.

All of these VA's are in the Philippines and charge between $2 - $7 per hour to work. I suggest hiring one or two VA's at a time is due to training. You have to prepare a call script for these new hires. They need to know what is expected of them. See the call script example below.

Call Script

Company: Multitude Investments, LLC
Title: Sales Manager
Location: Georgia, Texas & California

"Hi my name is (Your Name). I am calling to speak with (Name of Seller). The reason for my call today is to ask if you are interested in selling your property @ (Property Address?

If they respond (YES):
"Great, I will have a member from our acquisitions team follow up with you shortly. Is this the best number to reach you at? Also, can I have your email address? Thank you for your time!"

If they respond (NO):
"Ok no problem. Do you have any other properties you maybe interested in selling?

If (NO):
Ask are you a real estate investor?

If (YES):
Great, I will have a member from my acquisitions team reach out shortly. Is this the best number to reach you at? Also, can I have you email address?

Side Note:
If they ask how did you get my number? Answer,

"From the public directory & If you're not interested in selling I will remove your number from our call list, Thank you!"

You also have to prepare a Job Duties form as seen below.

MULTITUDE INVESTMENTS

Real Estate: Sales Representative

Job Description:
The Sales Representative attracts potential Sellers by making outbound phone calls. Document leads for those Sellers who expressed their interest to sell their property. Prepare clear documentation in the excel spreadsheet for the Sales Acquisitions Team to follow up to ensure a sale of the property.

Requires a high school diploma or equivalent and 0-3 years of experience in the field or in a related area. Will report to a designated Acquisitions Manager. The target is to follow the call script and make contact with 45 – 60 sellers per hour to gain the most seller leads possible.

Job functions:
- Document in each seller lead on the spreadsheet
- Manage large amounts of outbound calls
- Generate sales leads
- Identify and assess seller who want to sell their property
- Provide accurate, valid and complete information by using the right methods/tools
- Meet personal/team sales targets and call handling quotas of making contact with 45 – 60 sellers per hour.
- Document records of seller interactions
- Follow communication procedures, guidelines and policies
- Go the extra mile to engage customers
- Use personal telephones to reach out to customers
- Greet customers warmly and ascertain problem or reason for calling
- Read from scripts
- Handle changes in policies or renewals

Requirements:
- Proven customer support experience
- Track record of over-achieving quota
- Strong phone contact handling skills and active listening
- Familiar with CRM systems and practices
- Customer orientation and ability to adapt/respond to different types of characters
- Excellent communication and presentation skills
- Ability to multi-task, prioritize and manage time effectively
- High school diploma or equivalent; college degree preferred

Customer service representative top skills & proficiencies:
- Documentation Skills
- Listening Skills
- Phone Skills
- Multitask
- Positive Attitude
- Attention to Detail
- Adaptability
- Computer Skills

After you schedule your Skype interview and select a VA, I would recommend thoroughly training your initial VA's of your entire process. Including making outbound calls and also scheduling appointments. This will be helpful when you want to add more VA's to make calls. If you have trained your first VA's correctly and they have settled into your system well, they will be able to train your new VA's. Therefore you only have to go over training once with your initial VA's. It would be wise to give them a managerial title with an increase. This way the newer VA's will see there is potential for growth within your business. This incentive usually produces great results.

Step 4.) Identify Motivated Seller

Identifying your motivated seller is easily done when you apply the 4D's rule we discussed last chapter. Schedule your property visit. Here is a trick with the property visit you can apply once you establish a relationship with your buyers. Sometimes I do not go to the property at all. I cannot tell you how many properties I have sold that I never visited the property, met the owner or the buyer. This usually happen on vacant properties. It sounds impossible, I know. This game is all about how you communicate with each party. I always encourage the seller to place a key at the property or in a lockbox. You don't want your buyer and seller at the property without your presence. So I make sure the seller is unavailable the day I send my buyer to the vacant property on lock box. I will usually ask the seller what days are they free to be at the property. Usually weekends work best, therefore my buyers will only be scheduled to go visit Tuesday – Thursday 10am – 3pm. Most of your end buyers work for themselves or do not work a normal 9-5 job. A lot of time you will not have multiple chances to enter the property so I try to get my best buyer scheduled the same day the property is available for me to inspect. It is important that you take pictures every time you get access into the property. Advise the tenant or SMS that you must take pictures to get estimated quotes for possible upgrades once the home is purchased. This explanation is usually enough to bring their guard down. Next, inquire with your SMS on why they want to sell. Remember the 4D's, this is the point they will tell you one of the four main reasons each seller wants to sell. From there negotiations start. Always advise them your investors are cash buyers and can close as soon as title is clear which usually takes about 2weeks for CLEAN title. Dirty title can take much longer. Dirty title is the reason I tell people "DO NOT COUNT THE MONEY UNTIL THE WIRE HITS". Dirty title is a common used term for title with tons of liens, judgments, etc on the home or owner themselves. A good title agent can help avoid this if they know information upfront. However, you can see if the home has outstanding liens by pulling the property public county records. Anyone can search this information as long as you have the address. This will help you avoid bad deals especially vacant/abandoned homes. It's nice to know what you're getting into before you start the title process.

Step 5.) Put Under Contract

Now it's time to put the property under contract with your SMS. Contracts are probably the single most important thing in this wholesale business. As a wholesaler, you are not representing the seller or buyer in the transaction as a realtor or broker. You are simply assigning the rights of your contract to your end buyer. It is very important that you protect your self on both ends so you don't end up with a lawsuit.

Step 6.) Clear Title

Remember, every real estate transaction is governed by state laws and must be closed with a Real Estate attorney's title office. With that being said, you should know which closing attorney or title office to use for your transactions. You need to call the title company and ask if they accept assignment of contracts. Some may not even know what that is and that is a red flag that they are not "investor friendly". Typically those title companies deal solely with traditional closings, which are fine, but it's not a good fit for you as a wholesaler. You want a title company who is familiar with wholesale transactions. The assignment of contract is how you get paid so I think any genius would agree this is the most important piece of the business.

Step 7.) Find Buyer

If you are new to this business you probably want to know "where am I suppose to find buyers?" Yes, this was a hard process for me in the beginning too. There are a few ways to meet new buyers. One way to find buyers is to reach out to family and friends who may know someone who is into Real Estate. Another smart way is to find real estate meet ups to attend. Face book has tons of Real Estate groups; I can say I have had success using all three of these strategies. However, my first buyers were not your typical end buyers. When I closed my first $30k deal within the first 4 months, I used an acquisition company. These companies were formed during the 2008 - 2009 US Economy recession. They are backed by privately funded lenders & are staffed with licensed realtors who all work under a broker. Here is the catch; they do not represent any of their buyers or sellers as a realtor or broker even though they are licensed to do so. Instead they use their private owned lender to fund any deal they get under contract and resell it to their buyer. They do not close on many deals if they do not have a secured buyer. What does all of this mean right? Well it means they are glorified wholesalers too. Yes, the major hard money lending companies own glorified wholesale real estate companies and most people have no clue. A buddy of mine who worked for one of those companies once told me "If I knew I could wholesale Real Estate without having a realtor license, I would have never got a license". Working with these companies for the majority of my first couple years, taught me every dirty trick that people will play against you in Real Estate. Let me say this; do not deal with these guys if you are not ready, because they are trained sharks! They have unlimited buying power and have top tier lawyers ready to fight any lawsuit filed against them. Trust me, they get a lot of lawsuits. They win them all because their contracts are airtight. I have always been someone who like to work with the bad guys everyone else say don't work with. Here is a fun fact; I closed all of my biggest deals with those guys. The reason I was successful with them is because I'm a natural shark and love to compete with the best. The top acquisition companies are New Western and Net Worth. They were once the same company (New Western) until the leaders split creating Net Worth.

Step 8.) Close the Deal

Final step is to close the deal and receive either check or wire deposit. My preference is receiving payment via wire transfer. I suggest you create a domestic limited liability company (LLC). It's ok if you don't have it when you first get started.

I didn't either. It took eight months before I decided to file my LLC (Multitude Investments). I chose my company name because when I would cold call, I would often be asked by a PMS "What do you plan to do with the property"? My reply was "There are a multitude of things I can do with the property". Then Multitude Investments was born. So take some time to find a name that fits you and go for it.

Chapter 5.

Contract Agreements

"Your contracts should always be air tight on both sides of the deal"

In this chapter we will discuss the four types of contracts that you will need to run a successful wholesale business.

1.) Purchase and Sale Agreement with Seller

2.) Assignment of Contract

3.) Purchase and Sale Agreement with Buyer (aka Double Close)

4.) Joint Venture Agreement (aka JV Agreement)

5.) Marketing Agreement

Purchase and Sale Agreement with Seller

Keep it simple, is the basis of my Purchase and Sale Agreement (PSA). Most of the PMS or SMS are not savvy when it comes to real estate contracts. Most realtors' use the state issued single-family purchase agreement, which are very good from a legal standpoint. However, I use a very simple three-page contract (3rd page is signature page) that a 5th grader could understand every word in the contract. Always remember, "Less is more". Take a look at the PSA example.

REAL ESTATE PURCHASE AGREEMENT

MULTITUDE INVESTMENTS, LLC ("Buyer") agrees to buy, and OWNER ON RECORD ("Seller") agrees to sell, the real and personal property described below (the "Property"):

1. **Description.** The Property is described as follows:

   Address: 8129 Malone St Douglasville, GA 30134

   Personal property included with the real estate being sold: "AS IS"

2. **Purchase Price.** The purchase price is $ 225,000 , which shall be paid in cash at the closing. The earnest money described below shall be a credit against the purchase price.

3. **Closing Agent.** The closing agent shall be **CHALKER & CHALKER**. The closing agent shall disburse the earnest money at the closing and perform any other duties agreed in writing among Buyer, Seller, and the closing agent. The closing agent shall not be liable, except for gross negligence or intentional misconduct, for any matter related to the performance of duties in connection with this Agreement.

4. **Earnest Money.** Buyer has paid to the closing agent a deposit of $ 2,000 toward the purchase price. If there is an inspection period, Buyer will deposit earnest money within 48hrs after inspection period completed. If this earnest money has been paid by a check that is not honored by the bank upon which it is drawn, Buyer shall have 48 hours after written notice from the closing agent to deliver good funds to the closing agent. If Buyer does not do so, Seller shall have the right to terminate this Agreement upon written notice to Buyer.

5. **Closing.** This transaction shall be closed on **SEPTEMBER 26, 2019** at NOON a.m./p.m. at the office of the closing agent. If Seller cannot provide clear title by the close date above, this contract serves as an automatic 90 Business Days amendment between Buyer and Seller with no additional contract needed for signature. Real estate taxes, rents, dues, fees, and expenses relating to the Property for the year in which the sale is closed shall be prorated as of the date of closing. Taxes for prior years shall be paid by Seller.

6. **Closing Costs.** Seller shall pay all existing debt affecting the Property. Buyer shall pay all closing cost and escrow fees.

7. **Title Insurance.** Title insurance is not required.

8. **Financial Contingency.** This Agreement is not conditioned upon Buyer's ability to obtain a loan or any other financial contingency.

9. **Warranty Deed.** At the time of closing, Seller shall convey the Property by general warranty deed, subject only to the following on the date of closing: (a) governmental zoning and other ordinances and regulations; (b) utility, sewer, drainage, and other easements and stipulations; (c) subdivision and condominium covenants, conditions, declarations, and other restrictions; and (d) rights of tenants or claims of tenants in possession under oral, or written but unrecorded, leases or other agreements.

10. **Inspection.** Buyer shall be entitled to __14__ day inspection and have full access to property to show partners, lenders, inspectors and/or contractors at any time during inspection.

11. **Default.** Should Seller default, the earnest money shall be refunded to the Buyer.

12. **Binding Effect of this Agreement.** This Agreement shall be for the benefit of, and be binding upon, the parties, their heirs, successors, legal representatives and assigns. It constitutes the entire agreement between the parties. No modification of this Agreement shall be binding unless signed by both Buyer and Seller.

13. **Right To Termination.** Buyer has an unrestricted right to terminate this contract at any time prior to closing date.

14. **Cooperation.** Buyer and Seller agree to take promptly all actions reasonably necessary to carry out the responsibilities and obligations of this Agreement.

15. **Risk of Loss.** The risk of casualty loss or damage to the Property shall be borne by the Seller until transfer of title. If a casualty loss prior to closing exceeds 10% of the purchase price, either Seller or Buyer may elect to terminate this Agreement with a refund of earnest money to Buyer.

16. **Assignment.** This Agreement shall bind and inure to the benefit of the Seller and Buyer and their respective heirs, executors, administrators, personal and legal representatives, successors and permitted assigns. Buyer may assign Buyer's rights and responsibilities under this Agreement without the consent of the Seller.

17. **Other Terms.** The following terms and conditions supplement or supersede other provisions of this Agreement:

18. **Real Estate Commissions.** Neither party is represented by a real estate agent. If a real estate commission is asserted, the party whose conduct gave rise to the claim shall defend it and hold the other party harmless from any liability or expense arising from it.

19. **Effective Date.** This Agreement shall take effect on the later of the dates below.

20. **Governing Law.** This Agreement shall be interpreted in accordance with the laws of
GEORGIA

SELLERS:

Date: _____   _____   _____
                           Printed Name   Signature

Date: _____   _____   _____
                           Printed Name   Signature

BUYER:

Date: 8/20/19   MULTITUDE
                          INVESTMENTS, LLC   CEDRIC WILCOXSON
                          Name   Signature

REAL ESTATE PURCHASE AGREEMENT   PAGE 3

Assignment of Contract

This is the single most important contract you want to make sure you have signed by your buyer and submit to title. This contract is how you get paid! In wholesale real estate you are paid the difference of the purchase price with the seller and price you assigned the contract for. You get paid what you can negotiate. There is no ceiling on how much you can make. See example.

Assignment of Contract for Sale and Purchase of Real Estate

This Assignment is made and entered into effect as of the 24 day of MARCH, 2018 between Multitude Investments, LLC (ASSIGNOR) and Texas Mutual LLC (ASSIGNEE), regarding the real property described as:

LOT _____, BLOCK _____, ADDITION _____

ADDRESS 6008 Samcar Trail, Dallas, TX 75241

_____ (SUBJECT PROPERTY)

WHEREAS, the Assignor, as Buyer, entered into a Purchase and Sale Agreement with kermit sneed (SELLER) for the purchase of Subject Property for the amount of $ 80,000 (Subject Property Purchase Price), and whereas, Assignor wishes to assign its rights and interests in the Purchase and Sale Agreement, Assignor and Assignee hereby agree as follows:

I. **Assignment Fee**: Assignee shall pay Assignor an Assignment Fee in the amount of $ 7,000, which shall be collected on the settlement statement. Subject Property Purchase Price plus Assignment Fee to equal $ 87,000. The Assignment Fee is not earned if the purchase of the Subject Property does not close for any reason.

II. **Termination Period**: Assignor grants Assignee the unrestricted right to terminate this Assignment by giving Assignor notice of termination within 2 days after the execution of this Assignment. Assignee will deposit $ 3,000 earnest money with (X) the settlement agent/title company or ( ) Assignor to be held in escrow toward the Assignment Fee in paragraph I ( ) at time of execution of this Assignment or (X) at the expiration of the Termination Period. If Assignee terminates within the prescribed time or if the purchase of the Subject Property does not close for any reason, any earnest money paid by Assignee will be returned to Assignee.

III. **Closing Date**: Closing is to take place on or before March 30, 2018.

IV. **Contract for Sale and Purchase Acknowledgment**: Assignee accepts *all terms and conditions* of the original Contract for Sale and Purchase between Buyer and Seller. Assignee acknowledges receipt of legible copies of the original Contract for Sale and Purchase in its entirety including all addenda associated with this transaction.

V. **Ownership and Property Access Acknowledgment**: At the time of this Assignment, Assignor owns a Contract for Sale and Purchase of Subject Property. Assignor does not own title to Subject Property. Assignor and affiliated associates authorize Assignee to enter onto Subject Property upon their approval for inspections and due diligence. Assignor shall provide (1) all Seller's disclosures and contact information and (2) any other documents executed by Seller and Assignor to Assignee at time of execution of this Assignment.

VI. **Additional Disclosures and Acknowledgments**:

   a. **Real Estate Brokerage Disclosure**: Assignee acknowledges it is conducting a transaction directly with the Assignor for the purchase of the Subject Property. Assignor is not relying upon or being represented by a real estate brokerage in this transaction. Assignee is a licensed real estate agent.

   b. **Earnest Money and Option fee reimbursements**: Assignee acknowledges that any earnest and option monies disbursed by Assignor for the purchase of the Subject Property are to be reimbursed to the Assignor by Assignee on the HUD-1 Settlement Statement.

VII. **Additional terms and conditions of this Assignment are as follows**:

AGREED AND ACCEPTED:

Assignor: Multitude Investments, LLC

Signature: Andria Wilcoxson
Date: 3/24/2018
Address:
Phone:
Email:

Assignee: Texan Mutual LLC

Signature: [signature]
Date: 3/26/2018
Address:
Phone:
Email:

Purchase and Sale Agreement with Buyer

This contract is used for larger deals exceeding $10k. You never want to risk an investor pulling out of a deal because of how much you are making on your assignment fee. So to be safe, we will double close the larger deals. At least do so until you have established a relationship with your end buyer. This should be applied case by case. In real estate, no deal is ever the same. The factors are always different. You would still write this PSA the same way you did for the seller, however this time you will sign as the seller with your end buyer. I have provided an example.

REAL ESTATE PURCHASE AGREEMENT

RBA PROPERTIES, LLC ("Buyer") agrees to buy, and **MULTITUDE INVESTMENTS, LLC** ("Seller") agrees to sell, the real and personal property described below (the "Property"):

1. **Description.** The Property is described as follows:

   Address: **8129 Malone St Douglasville, GA 30134**

   Personal property included with the real estate being sold: "NO IO"

2. **Purchase Price.** The purchase price is $ **239,000**, which shall be paid in cash at the closing. The earnest money described below shall be a credit against the purchase price.

3. **Closing Agent.** The closing agent shall be **CHALKER & CHALKER**. The closing agent shall disburse the earnest money at the closing and perform any other duties agreed in writing among Buyer, Seller, and the closing agent. The closing agent shall not be liable, except for gross negligence or intentional misconduct, for any matter related to the performance of duties in connection with this Agreement.

4. **Earnest Money.** Buyer has paid to the closing agent a deposit of $ **3,000** toward the purchase price. If there is an inspection period, Buyer will deposit earnest money at the time of execution of this purchase agreement. If this earnest money has been paid by a check that is not honored by the bank upon which it is drawn, Seller shall have the right to terminate this Agreement upon written notice to Buyer.

5. **Closing.** This transaction shall be closed on **SEPTEMBER 9, 2019** at **NOON** a.m./p.m. at the office of the closing agent. Real estate taxes, rents, dues, fees, and expenses relating to the Property for the year in which the sale is closed shall be prorated as of the date of closing. Taxes for prior years shall be paid by Seller.

6. **Closing Costs.** Seller shall pay all existing debt affecting the Property. Buyer shall pay all closing cost and escrow fees.

7. **Title Insurance.** Title insurance is required.

8. **Financial Contingency.** This Agreement is not conditioned upon Buyer's ability to obtain a loan or any other financial contingency.

9. **Warranty Deed.** At the time of closing, Seller shall convey the Property by general warranty deed, subject only to the following on the date of closing: (a) governmental zoning and other ordinances and regulations; (b) utility, sewer, drainage, and other easements and stipulations; (c) subdivision and condominium covenants, conditions, declarations, and other restrictions; and (d) rights of tenants or claims of tenants in possession under oral, or written but unrecorded, leases or other agreements.

10. **Inspection.** Buyer has inspected the property and is buying property "As Is".

11. **Default.** Should Seller default, the earnest money shall be refunded to the Buyer. Should Buyer default, earnest money will not be refunded.

12. **Binding Effect of this Agreement.** This Agreement shall be for the benefit of, and be binding upon, the parties, their heirs, successors, legal representatives and assigns. It constitutes the entire agreement between the parties. No modification of this Agreement shall be binding unless signed by both Buyer and Seller.

13. **Cooperation.** Buyer and Seller agree to take promptly all actions reasonably necessary to carry out the responsibilities and obligations of this Agreement.

14. **Risk of Loss.** The risk of casualty loss or damage to the Property shall be borne by the Seller until transfer of title. If a casualty loss prior to closing exceeds 10% of the purchase price, either Seller or Buyer may elect to terminate this Agreement with a refund of earnest money to Buyer.

15. **Real Estate Commissions.** Neither party is represented by a real estate agent. If a real estate commission is asserted, the party whose conduct gave rise to the claim shall defend it and hold the other party harmless from any liability or expense arising from it.

16. **Effective Date.** This Agreement shall take effect on the later of the dates below.

17. **Governing Law.** This Agreement shall be interpreted in accordance with the laws of GEORGIA.

18. **Contingency.** Seller has to provide Buyer copies of lease agreements, specific rent roll payment history and contact information for Section 8 division. If Seller fails to provide this information by September 4, 2019 Buyer can terminate contract upon written notice to seller.

SELLERS:

Date: 09/01/19

MULTITUDE INVESTMENTS, LLC
Printed Name

CEDRIC WILCOXSON
Signature

Date: _____

_____
Printed Name

_____
Signature

BUYER:

Date: 9-3-19

Steve Brandt
Name

_____
Signature

Joint Venture Agreement

Joint Venture also known as JV Agreement is commonly used amongst wholesalers. Especially wholesalers who are new and do not have a large buyers list. Doing JV agreements is a good way to build your network with other wholesalers. Knowing how to structure your JV agreements is important. Typically I will do 50/50 spilt on JV agreements with another party. This means when the property is closed we would split the payout 50/50. I recommend only doing JV agreement with people who have a serious buyer or if they can provide you a copy of the original contract with the seller. Time is money and you do not want to do business with someone who cannot perform. In today's world I only do JV agreements with my real estate buddies who I have done several deals with if needed. The longer you're in the game the less JV deals you will do because you will increase your end buyer's list. See JV agreement example.

JV Agreement
JOINT VENTURE AGREEMENT AND MARKETING ADDENDUM

This agreement relates to the contract for the property/properties located at: 2831 Wilhurt Ave, 2633 Lea Crest Dr, 3046 Alabama Ave, 3027 Alabama Ave (Dallas, TX 75216) between Dennis Topletz/Fred Brewster and Cedric Wilcoxson /MULTITUDE INVESTMENTS, LLC.

Cedric Wilcoxson /MULTITUDE INVESTMENTS, LLC agrees to pay Make One Investment Group, LLC as a joint venture fee of $ 9,800 , at Closing for finding a motivated buyer as discussed.

[signature]
Payee Signature

Make One Investment Group, LLC
Printed Name

And

[signature]
Payer Signature

Cedric Wilcoxson /MULTITUDE INVESTMENTS, LLC
Print Name

Marketing Agreement

This agreement differs from the JV agreement simply because it is strictly for marketing purposes only. Meaning if the party who was given the task to market the property does not perform, then they do not receive payment at closing. Unlike the JV agreement, you are partners and both receive payment at closing regardless. I do use marketing agreements today with wholesalers who I have never worked with because I can cancel our agreement anytime if they do not secure an end buyer by a certain date. I would advise giving someone maximum 10 days on a marketing agreement. If they cannot secure a buyer within 10 days then they most likely do not have an end buyer interested. Please see marketing agreement example.

MARKETING FEE AGREEMENT

This addendum relates to the contract for the property located at:

Address: 975 - 979 Sparks St SW, Atlanta, GA 30310

Between: MULTITUDE INVESTMENTS, LLC

And: Southern State Investments LLC

Dated: 12/3/2020

Southern State Investments agrees to pay MULTITUDE INVESTMENTS, LLC $2,500 marketing/consulting fee at closing.

Cedric Wilcoxson	Cedric Wilcoxson	12/3/2020
Print Name	**Signature**	**Date**

Andre Grant	[signature]	12/3/2020
Print Name	**Signature**	**Date**

Summary

I hope this information has been useful and helps you grow a six-figure real estate business within your first year like I did. My sole intention was to inspire someone to be great in this wholesale business. Please note that wholesale real estate is a great introduction to real estate if you do not have much capital to buy and flip a home. Some people I started wholesaling with have earned their real estate license with the intent on having their own brokerage firm one day. Some have become full time fix and flippers and some entered returned to the corporate world. The idea is to have a plan for yourself and execute your plan. Do not hesitate to share this book with your family, friends and colleagues. This information should be shared. Thank you for your time.

"Always keep going & never stop"

References

1.) What is Wholesale Real Estate?

https://connectedinvestors.com/blog/wholesaling-houses-step-by-step/?wickedsource=google&wickedid=CjwKCAjw7diEBhB-EiwAskVi1xP3m0DaM0jSZ7E5BLLuFhMKewgC-aiddv8z2iifid02A1bE4rerBhoCLFEQAvD_BwE&wv=3&&gclid=CjwKCAjw7diEBhB-EiwAskVi1xP3m0DaM0jSZ7E5BLLuFhMKewgC-aiddv8z2iifid02A1bE4rerBhoCLFEQAvD_BwE

2.) https://www.investopedia.com/terms/o/one-percent-rule.asp

3.) https://www.biggerpockets.com/blog/70-percent-rule

Acknowledgement

Hearing so many people I know say they have wanted to get into real estate but did not know how, or did not have the money to invest inspired this book. Also witnessing family and friends pay enormous amount of money from "Real Estate Experts" just to be funneled into paying more money for free information. I wanted to provide a book that will help people. First I have to thank God for my life. I am thankful for the support of my parents (Amanda & Cedric Wilcoxson Sr.) throughout my entire life journey. This book would not have been possible if I was not introduced to real estate. Dr. Randy Bell introduced me into wholesale real estate in 2016 in Dallas, TX on the rooftop of a bar called "Happiest Hour" in Victory Park. I was amongst other friends but out of that group that night, I was the one who followed up on Randy's message about wholesale real estate. I like to say that Real Estate saved my life. Not in the literal sense but it gave me a sense of purpose and a career that I was in complete control of. There is nothing like being able to control your own income. My brother Jerry Davis always motivates me to stay consistent in this real estate business. I have to give credit to all of the people who have taken advice from me to get started in the real estate industry. I also want to thank Ms. Credit for helping me edit and proofread the final draft. My intention is for anyone who has contributed to my experiences and success in real estate to know that this book could not have been written without all of you. Thank you all again!

Review

This book is focused on giving away useful "information". We live in the information age, where so much information is easily accessible to everyone at our fingertip via smart phones. Major data platforms like Google, Yahoo and Bing have made it easy to become an expert at anything. Today you can learn how to do anything by video via You Tube. Real Estate is no different. There are tons of wholesale real estate platforms for people to get an understanding of what is wholesale real estate. What is not easily accessible is the information needed to startup your business. This book dives into the details needed to create your wholesale business from A-Z. Every person who wants to learn about the wholesale real estate business needs to read this short & insightful book. The right information is key to economic success.

Made in the USA
Columbia, SC
24 August 2021